Elias Howe

The Pianist's Social Circle

A Collection of Vocal and Instrumental Music for the Piano-Forte

Elias Howe

The Pianist's Social Circle
A Collection of Vocal and Instrumental Music for the Piano-Forte

ISBN/EAN: 9783337103668

Printed in Europe, USA, Canada, Australia, Japan

Cover: Foto ©Thomas Meinert / pixelio.de

More available books at **www.hansebooks.com**

THE PIANIST'S SOCIAL CIRCLE,

A COLLECTION OF

Vocal and Instrumental Music,

FOR THE

PIANO-FORTE,

CONSISTING OF

Songs and Ballads; Irish and Scotch Melodies; Waltzes, Galops, Polkas, Polka Redowas, Marches, Quicksteps, Quadrilles, Fancy and Contra Dances, with Calls, &c.

BY ELIAS HOWE.

BOSTON:
PUBLISHED AND SOLD BY ELIAS HOWE,
103 COURT STREET.

INDEX TO PIANIST'S SOCIAL CIRCLE.

INSTRUMENTAL.

Full Sets of Waltzes.

Quadrilles.

Galops, Polkas, Polka Redowas, etc.

Contra Dances, etc.

SONGS,

With Piano Accompaniment.

List to the Nightingale's Song.

Sweetly warbling o'er the billow,
  Flies a pretty little bird —
Music's charms shall sooth your pillow,
  Sweeter strains were never heard.
      Courage, brave hearts, &c.
Hark ! of golden hope she's singing —
  Warbling of celestial things,
Heavenly consolation bringing,
  Dropping balsam from her wings.
      Courage, brave hearts, &c.

Home, and wife, and children dear,
  In her melody you'll find —
Sorrow smiles with joy to hear
  Of the dear ones left behind.
And, though death may raise his dart,
  Still the Nighingale's sweet voice
Gently cheers the sinking heart,
  Bids the parting soul rejoice.
List to the Nightingale's song !

THE GOLDEN RING.

G. LINLEY.

THE GREEN LITTLE SHAMROCK.

2 This dear little plant still grows in our land,
Fresh and fair as the daughters of Erin;
Whose smiles can bewitch, whose eyes can command,
In each climate that each shall appear in.
And shine thro' the bog, thro' the brake, thro' the mire-land,
Just like their own dear little Shamrock of Ireland.
The sweet little Shamrock, &c.

3 This dear little plant that springs from our soil,
When its three little leaves are extended,
Denotes from our stalk we together should toil,
And ourselves by ourselves be befriended.
And still thro' the bog, thro' the brake, thro' the mire-land,
From one root should branch like the Shamrock of Ireland.
The sweet little Shamrock, &c.

MY MOTHER'S PORTRAIT.

2 Oft, oft when I gaze on those features so fair,
As mild as an angel's, upraised in prayer,
I fancy her eyes beam with fondness on me,
And my kind mother there, as in life, still I see.
She is shrin'd in my heart, but, alas! with a tear
I bedew the fair semblance I worship'd so here;
And turn from the world oft to utter a prayer,
And to look, unobserved, on that dear face there!

3 Sweet mother, in childhood you cradled my head,
And I pillowed thine when thou slept with the dead;
All, all my heart's treasures were centered in thee,
And for aye unforgotten thy mem'ry will be
The soft sweet voice that bless'd me falls now on mine ear,
And the hands that caressed me seem still to be near.
Tears shame not a man when a tear aids the prayer
That I breathe for the peace of that dear face there!

CAPTAIN JINKS.

3 The first day I went out to drill,
The bugle-sound made me quite ill;
At the balance-step, my hat it fell,
And that wouldn't do for the army.
The officers they all did shout,
They all cried out, they all did shout;
The officers they all did shout,
"Oh! that's the cure for the army."

SPOKEN. Of course, my hat did fall off; but ah! nevertheless.
CHORUS.

4 My tailor's bills came in so fast,
Forc'd me one day to leave at last;
And ladies too no more did cast
Sheep's eyes at me in the army.
My creditors at me did shout.
At me did shout, at me did shout;
My creditors at me did shout,
"Why, kick him out of the army."

SPOKEN. I said, ah! gentlemen, ah! kick me out of the army?
Perhaps you are not aware that— CHORUS.

I HEARD THE WEE BIRD SINGING.

GEORGE LINLEY.

2 He heard the wee bird singing,
For its notes were wond'rous clear;
As if wedding bells were ringing,
Melodious to the ear.
And still it rang, that wee bird's song,
Just like the bells, ding dong, ding dong;
While my heart beat time so quick and strong,
I felt that he was near;
‖: Ah! he heard that wee bird singing, :‖
That wee bird, that wee bird,
Ah! he heard that wee bird singing.

3 We heard the wee bird singing,
After many years had flown;
The true bells had been ringing,
And Willie was my own.
Oft strolling thro' the forest glade,
I mind him what the wee bird said,
That morn when he no longer stayed,
But flew to me alone.
‖: Oh! we love the wee bird singing, :‖
That wee bird, that wee bird,
Oh! we love the wee bird singing.

A THOUSAND GREETINGS TO OUR FRIENDS.

CHAMPAGNE CHARLIE.

MUSIC BY ALFRED LEE.

CHAMPAGNE CHARLIE. Another Version.

1 Some time ago. I had a beau,
And Charlie was his name;
A smart young fellow, fond of show,
Who wished my hand to claim;
But from my feet I spurned the swell,
As I will now explain.—
Although he liked me very well,
He better loved Champagne.

CHORUS.—For Champagne Charlie was his name,
Champagne Charlie was his name;
Always kicking up a frightful noise,
Always kicking up a frightful noise;
Champagne Charlie was his name,
Champagne Charlie was his name;
Kicking up a noise at night,
And always ready for a spree.

3 One moment still he couldn't rest,
He'd pass whole nights and days
In drinking Madam Cliquot's best,
And smoking "Henry Clay's."
Then when to bed he'd homeward go,
With wild disordered brain,
He'd lay it to his studies, tho'
I knew 'twas to Champagne! CHORUS.—

3 He promised me of times a score,
That he the pledge would take;
But acted just like many more,
And soon his word did break.
Yes, if for one half-day complete,
From drink he could abstain,
He'd go and resolution treat,
To his revered Champagne. CHORUS.—

4 He was an artist in his way,
Drew Herons, Cranes, and Storks;
Yet, for all that, he passed the day
In simply drawing corks.
Tho' he'd a palette for his paints,
To use it he'd not deign,
Because he'd like some other "saint,"
A palate for Champagne! CHORUS.—

5 His cash did quickly disappear.
Which did not well suit me;
For Champagne's dear — had he drank beer,
Things different now would be.
I might have been his slave for life,
But now 'tis all in vain;
For how can he require a wife,
When wedded to — Champagne! CHORUS.—

"OH, WOULD I WERE A BIRD."

C. BLAMPHIN.

AS I'D NOTHING ELSE TO DO.

J. L. HATTON.

3

Then we rambled forth together,
Down the lane, beneath the trees,
While so gently stirred the shadows
Of their branches in the breeze;
And whene'er our conversation
Languished for a word or two,
Why, of course, I kindly kissed her,
As I'd nothing else to do.

4

But, before the day was over,
I'd somehow made up my mind
That I'd pop the question to her,
If to me her heart inclined;
So I whisper'd, "Sweet, my darling,
Will you have me, Yes, or No?"
"Well," she said, "perhaps I may, my dear,
When I've nothing else to do."

"NOT FOR JOSEPH."

ARTHUR LLOYD.

1. Jo-seph Bax-ter is my name, My friends all call me Joe; I'm up, you know, to ev-'ry game, And ev-'ry-thing I know. Ah! I once was green as green could be; I suffer'd for it, though. Now, if they try it on with me, I tell them 'Not for Joe.'

2. I us'd to throw my cash a-bout In a reckless sort of way; I'm careful now what I'm a-bout, And cau-tious how I pay. Now, the other night I ask'd a pal, With me to have a drain,—"Thanks, Joe," said he, "let's see, old pal," "I think I'll have Champagne."
Will ye? said I: oh, no,—

'Not for Joe,' 'Not for Joe,' If he knows it; Not for Jo-seph, No, no, no. 'Not for Joe,' Not for Jo-seph, oh dear, no!

3

There's a fellow called Jack Dannister,
He's a sort of chap is Jack,
Who is always money borrowing,
And never pays ye back;
Now last Thursday night he came to me,
Said he'd just returned to town,
And was rather short of cash,—
Could I lend him half-a-crown?

Well, said I, if I thought I should get it back again, I would, with pleasure; but, excuse me if I say,—

'Not for Joe,' etc.

3

A friend of mine, down in Pall Mall,
The other night, said "Joe,
I'll introduce you to a gal
You really ought to know;
She's a widow you should try and win;
'Twould a good match be for you;
She's pretty, and got lots of tin,
And only forty-two.

Fancy forty-two, old enough to be my grand-mother, and you know a fella' can't marry his grand-mother; lots of tin, though, and pretty; forty-two! No,—

'Not for Joe,' etc.

THOSE TASSELS ON THE BOOTS.

1. 'Twas at a fan-cy ball.... I met a charmer fair, 'Midst waltzing swells and dashing belles, The pret-ti-est dancer there, I
p
watched her while the music played the latest waltz of Coote's, And fell in love, no, not with her, With those tassels on her boots, Oh! yes,
rall.
ral.
SPOKEN.—Yes through those little peep-holes in that pretty white petticoat, I could plainly see.—
CHORUS.
Those tassels on the boots, A style I'm sure that suits, Our Yankee girls with hair in curls, Those tassels on the boots.
mf
cresc.

2.

I watched her up the stairs,
Where we to supper went,
Upon those tassels on her boots,
My soul was so intent;
They asked me to propose a health,
Said I, "here's one that suits,
So fill your glasses up and drink
To the tassels on the boots."

SPOKEN.—I meant to drink to the ladies' healths, but I could think of nothing, but—

Those tassels on the boots, &c.

3.

I asked this girl "if I
Might call," she said "you may,
But tell me why you gaze upon
The ground in such a way?
You're sad perhaps, for life is full
Of very bitter fruits;"
"Oh no," I said, "I'm looking at
Those tassels on your boots."

SPOKEN.—What is a more lovely sight when you walk down Washington Street than to look at—

Those tassels on the boots, &c.

4.

I called on her next day,
And Cupid's cruel shoots,
Soon made me throw myself before
Those tassels on her boots; [got
Now when we're married and we've
A lot of little toots,
I'll make them, whether boys or girls,
Wear tassels on their boots.

SPOKEN.—If I were to have fifty children, they should every single one wear those pretty, pretty,—

Those tassels on the boots, &c.

KATE KEARNEY.

1. Oh! did you not hear of Kate Kear-ney, She lives on the banks of Kil-lar-ney, From the
glance of her eye, shun dan-ger and fly, For fa-tal's the glance of Kate Kear-ney.
For that eye is so mod-est-ly beam-ing, You'd ne'er think of mis-chief she's dream-ing, Yet
Oh! I can tell how fa-tal's the spell That lurks in the eye of Kate Kear-ney.

2

Oh! should you e'er meet with Kate Kearney,
Who lives on the banks of Killarney,
Beware of her smile, for many a wile
Lies hid in the smile of Kate Kearney.

Tho' she looks so bewitchingly simple,
Yet there's mischief in every dimple,
And who dares inhale her sigh's spicy gale,
Must die by the breath of Kate Kearney.

3 Then come along with me,
Gramachree, and you'll see
How happy you will be,
With your bowld sojer boy;
Faith if you're up to fun,
With me run, 'twill be done
In the snapping of a gun,
Says the bowld sojer boy.

And 'tis then that without scandal,
Myself will proudly dandle
The little farthing candle
Of our mutual flame, my joy;
May his light shine as bright as mine,
'Till in the line he'll blaze and raise
The glory of his corps,
Like a bowld sojer boy.

SHALL THE HARP THEN BE SILENT.

3. What a union of all the affections and powers
   By which life is exalted, embellished, refined,
Was embraced in that spirit—whose centre was ours,
   While its mighty circumference circled mankind.

4. O, who that loves Erin, or who that can see,
   Through the waste of her annals, that epoch sublime—
Like a pyramid raised in the desert—where he
   And his glory stand out to the eyes of all time;

5. That *one* lucid interval, snatched from the gloom
   And the madness of ages, when filled with his soul,
A Nation o'erleaped the dark bounds of her doom,
   And for *one* sacred instant, touched Liberty's goal?

6. Who, that ever hath heard him—hath drunk at the source
   Of that wonderful eloquence, all Erin's own,
In whose high-thoughted daring, the fire, and the force,
   And the yet untamed spring of her spirit are shown?

7. An eloquence rich, wheresoever it wave,
   Wander'd free and triumphant, with tho'ts that shone thro',
As clear as the brook's "stone of lustre," and gave
   With the flash of the gem, its solidity too.

8. Who, that ever approached him, when free from the crowd,
   In a home full of love, he delighted to tread
'Mong the trees which a nation had given, and which bowed,
   As if each brought a new civic crown for his head—

9. Is there one, who hath thus, through his orbit of life,
   But at distance observed him—through glory, through blame,
In the calm of retreat, in the grandeur of strife,
   Whether shining or clouded, still high and the same,—

10. O, no, not a heart, that e'er knew him, but mourns
   Deep, deep o'er the grave, where such glory is shrined—
O'er a monument Fame will preserve, 'mong the urns
   Of the wisest, the bravest, the best of mankind!

WIDOW MACHREE.

2. Widow Machree, now the summer is come,
Och hone, Widow Machree;
When everything smiles, should a beauty look glum?
Och hone, Widow Machree;
See the birds go in pairs,
And the rabbits and hares,—
Why, even the bears
Now in couples agree;
And the mute little fish,
Though they can't speak, they wish,
Och hone, Widow Machree.

3. Widow Machree, and when winter comes in,
Och hone, Widow Machree;
To be poking the fire all alone is a sin,
Och hone, Widow Machree;
Why the shovel and tongs
To each other belongs,
And the kettle sings songs,
Full of family glee;
While alone with your cup,
Like a hermit you sup,
Och hone, Widow Machree.

4. And how do you know with the comforts I've told,
Och hone, Widow Machree;
But you're keeping some poor fellow out in the cold?
Och hone, Widow Machree;
With such sins on your head,
Sure your peace would be fled,
Could you sleep in your bed
Without thinking to see
Some ghost or some sprite,
That would wake you each night,
Crying, "och hone, Widow Machree?"

5. Then take my advice, darlin' Widow Machree,
Och hone, Widow Machree;
And with my advice, faith, I'd wish you'd take me,
Och hone, Widow Machree;
You'd have me to desire,
Then to stir up the fire,
And sure hope is no liar,
In whispering to me;
That the ghosts would depart,
When you'd me near my heart.
Och hone, Widow Machree.

ANGEL'S WHISPER.

S. Lover.

A superstition of great beauty prevails in Ireland, that when a child smiles in its sleep, it is talking to angels.

ANDANTE. Molto espressione.

A

ba - by was sleeping, Its moth - er was weeping, For her hus - band was far on the

wild raging sea, And the tem - pest was swelling, Round the fisher - man's dwelling, And she

f Cres. Ad lib. Colla voce.

Feelingly.

cried, "Der - mot dar - ling, Oh come back to me." Her

2.
And while they are keeping
Bright watch o'er thy sleeping,
Oh, pray to them softly,
My baby with me,
And say thou would'st rather
They'd watch o'er thy Father,
For I know that the angels
Are whispering with thee.

3.
The dawn of the morning
Saw Dermot returning,
And the wife wept with joy
Her babe's father to see,
And closely caressing
Her child, with a blessing,
Said, "I know that the angels
Were whispering with thee."

THE FAIRY BOY.

S. Lover.

When a beautiful child pines and dies, the Irish peasant believes the healthy infant has been stolen by the fairies, and a sickly Elf left in its place.

J. Parry.

Moderato con Espressivo.
1. As beauteous as Flora is charming young Norah, The joy of my heart, and the pride of Kildare; I
2. Where e'er I may be, love, I'll ne'er for-get thee, love! Though beauties may smile and try to en-snare; Yet
mf
ne'er can deceive her, For sadly t'would grieve her, To find that I sighed for a-nother less fair. Her
noth-ing shall ev-er thy heart from mine sev-er, Dear Norah, sweet No-rah, the pride of Kildare. Her
heart with truth teeming, Her eyes with smiles beaming; What mor-tal could in-jure a blossom so rare, As
heart with truth teeming, Her eyes with smiles beaming; What mor-tal could in-jure a blossom so rare, As
No-rah, dear No-rah, the pride of Kildare, As No-rah, dear No-rah, the pride of Kildare.

'TIS THE LAST ROSE OF SUMMER.

T. Moore.

KITTY TYRRELL.

Words by Charles Jefferys. Music by C. W. Glover.

RORY O'MOORE.

Words and Arrangement by S. Lover.

2 "Indeed then," says Kathleen, "dont't think of the like,
For I half gave a promise to soothering Mike;
The ground that I walk on he loves, I'll be bound,"
"Faith," says Rory, "I'd rather love you than the ground."
"Now Rory, I'll cry if you don't let me go,
Sure I dream every night that I'm hating you so!"
"O," says Rory, "that same I'm delighted to hear,
For dhrames always go by conthrairies my dear;
O, Jewel, keep dreaming that same till you die,
And bright morning will give dirty night the black lie;
And 'tis pleased that I am, and why not to be sure?
Since 'tis all for good luck," says bold Rory O'Moore.

3 Arrah Kathleen, my darlint, you've teazed me enough,
And I've thrash'd for your sake Dinny Grimes and Jim Duff,
And I've made myself drinking your health quite a baste,
So I think, after that, I may TALK TO THE PRIEST." *
Then Rory, the rogue, stole his arm round her neck,
So soft and so white, without freckle or speck,
And he looked in her eyes, that were beaming with light,
And he kissed her sweet lips—don't you think he was right?
"Now Rory, leave off sir, you'll hug me no more,
That's eight times to-day that you've kissed me before;"
"Then here goes another," says he, "to make sure,
For there's luck in odd numbers," says Rory O'Moore.

* Paddy's mode of asking a girl to name the day.

BIRTH OF ST. PATRICK.

1. On the eighth day of March it was, some peo - ple say, That St. Patrick at midnight he first saw the day: While
oth - ers de - clare 'twas the ninth he was born, And 'twas all a mis - take between midnight and morn: For mis-
- takes will oc - cur in a hur - ry and shock, And some blam'd the ba - by, and some blam'd the clock, 'Till
with all their cross questions sure no one could know If the child was too fast, or the clock was too slow.

2. Now the first faction fought in ould Ireland, they say,
Was all on account of Saint Patrick's birthday,
Some fought for the eighth—for the ninth more would die,
And both would'nt see right, sure they blacken'd his eye!
At last both the factions as positive grew,
That each kept a birthday—so Pat then had two,
'Till Father Mulcahy, who showed them their sins,
Said "no one could have two birthdays but a pair of twins."

3. Says he, "boys don't be fighting for eight or for nine,
Don't always be dividing—but sometimes combine;
Combine eight with nine, and seventeen is the mark,
So let that be his birthday." "Amen," says the clerk.
"If he was'nt a twin, sure our hist'ry will show—
That, at least, he is worth two saints that we know!"
Then they all got blind drunk—which completed their bliss,
And we kept up the practice from that day to this.

KATHLEEN MAVOURNEEN.

KATHLEEN MAVOURNEEN. Concluded.
- - - got-ten this day we must part. It may be for years, and it may be for -
Colla voce.
- ev-er. Oh, why art thou si-lent, thou voice of my heart. It may be for
years, and it may be for - ov-er, Then why art thou si-lent, Kath-leen Ma-vour-neen.
Cres.
mf
p
2.
Kathleen Mavourneen, awake from thy slumbers,
The blue mountains glow in the sun's golden light,
Ah! where is the spell that once hung on my numbers,
Arise in thy beauty, thou star of my sight.
Mavourneen, Mavourneen, my sad tears are falling,
To think that from Erin and thee I must part;
It may be for years, and it may be forever,
Then why art thou silent, thou voice of my heart;
It may be for years, and it may be forever,
Then why art thou silent, Kathleen Mavourneen.
FAGAN.
IRISH DANCE.
mf
f

KITTY OF COLERAINE.

2.

I then walk'd beside her, and gently did chide her,
That such a misfortune should give her such pain;
A kiss then I gave her, and ere I did leave her,
She blush'd and consent'ed to meet me again.

'Twas haymaking season—I can't tell the reason—
Mis-fortunes will never come single, 'tis plain;
For very soon after poor Kitty's disaster,
The devil a pitcher was whole in Coleraine.

WIDOW MALONE.

2. " Of lovers she had a full score,
Or more;
And fortunes they all had galore,
In store;
From the minister down
To the clerk of the town
All were courting the Widow Malone
Ohone,
All were courting the Widow Malone.

3. " But so modest was Mrs. Malone,
'Twas known
No one ever could see her alone,
Ohone!
Let them ogle and sigh,
They could ne'er catch her eye,
So bashful the Widow Malone,
Ohone!
So bashful the Widow Malone.

4. " Till one Mister O'Brien from Clare,
How quare!
It's little for blushin' they care
Down there;
Put his arm round her waist,
Gave ten kisses, at laste,
'Oh!' says he, 'you're my Molly Malone,
My own;'
'Oh!' says he, 'you're my Molly Malone.'

5. The Widow they all thought so shy,
My eye!
Ne'er thought of a simper or sigh,
For why?
But Luctus; says she,
'Since you've made now so free,
You may marry your Mary Malone,
Ohone!
You may marry your Mary Malone.'

6. " There's a moral contained in my song,
Not wrong;
And one comfort it's not very long
But strong;
If for Widows you die,
Larn to Kiss, not Sigh;
For they're all like sweet Mistress Malone,
Ohone!
For they're all like sweet Mistress Malone."

LOONEY MACTWOLTER.

1. Oh, whack! Cu - pid's a man - ni - kin, Smack on my back he hit me a pol - ter; Good lack!
Ju - dy O'-Flan-ni - kin! Dearly she loves neat Loo - ney Mactwol - ter. Judy's my darling, my kis - ses she suffers; She's an
heiress, that's clear, For her fa - ther sells beer; He keeps the sign of the Cow and the Snuffers. She's so smart, From my heart
I can - not bolt her. Oh, whack! Ju - dy O' - Flan - ni - kin! She is the girl for Loo - ney Mac - twol - ter.

2. Och hone! good news I need a bit;
We'd correspond, but learning would choke her:
Mavrone! I cannot read a bit;
Judy can't tell a pen from a poker.
Judy's so constant I'll never forsake her;
She's as true as the moon,
Only one afternoon
I caught the jilt kissing a hump-back'd shoemaker;
Oh, she's smart! From my heart
I cannot bolt her.
Oh, whack! Judy O'Flannikin!
She's the girl for Looney Mactwolter.

OH! STEER MY BARK TO ERIN'S ISLE.

1. Oh! I have roam'd in ma - ny lands, And ma - ny friends I've met; Not
one fair scene or kind - ly smile, Can this fond heart for - get. But I'll con - fess that
I'm con - tent, No more I wish to roam; Oh steer my bark to E - rin's Isle, For
E - rin is my home, Oh! steer my bark to E - rin's Isle, For E - rin is my home.
p
f

2.

If England were my place of birth,
I'd love her tranquil shore;
If bonny Scotland were my home,
Her mountains I'd adore.

Though pleasant days in both I pass,
I dream of days to come;
Oh steer my bark to Erin's Isle,
For Erin is my home.

SHULE AGRAH, OR JOHNNY HAS GONE FOR A SOLDIER.

2. Some say my love has gone to France,
There his fortune to advance,
And if I find him, its but a chance,
Oh, Johnny has gone for a soldier.
Shule, shule, &c.

3. I'll sell my flax, I'll sell my wheel,
I'll buy my love a sword of steel,
So in the battle he may reel,
Oh, Johnny has gone for a soldier.
Shule, shule, &c.

4. I wish I was on yonder hill,
It's there I'd sit and cry my fill,
So every tear may turn a mill,—
Oh, Johnny has gone for a soldier.
Shule, shule, &c.

5. I'll dye my dress, I'll dye it red,
And through the streets I'll beg my bread.
Oh, how I wish that I was dead,
Since Johnny has gone for a soldier.
Shule, &c.

DUBLIN BAY.

1. There sail'd a - way in a gal - lant ship, Roy Neill and his fair young bride, They had
ven - tur'd all in the bound - ing barque that danc'd o'er the silv' - ry tide; But
their hearts were young and spir'ts light, As they dash'd the tears a - way, As they
watch'd the shore re - cede from sight of their own sweet "Dub - lin Bay."

2.

Three days they sailed, when a storm arose, and lightning flash'd the deep,
And the thunder's crash, broke the short repose of the weary seamen's sleep.
Roy Neill he clasped his weeping bride, and kissed her tears away,
'Oh, love,' she cried, ' 'twas a fatal hour we left sweet Dublin Bay.'

3.

On the crowded deck of the doomed ship, some knelt in mute despair,
While some, more calm, with a holy lip rais'd their voice to their God in pra'r;
She's struck on the rocks, the sailors cried; in the depth of their wild dismay,
The ship went down with that fair young bride that sail'd from Dublin Bay.

SAINT PATRICK WAS GENTLEMAN.

2. There's not a mile in Ireland's Isle, where the dirty varmin musters,
Where'er he put his dear forehad, he murder'd them in clusters.
The Toads went hop, the Frogs went flop, slap dash into the water,
And the beasts committed Suicide to save themselves from slaughter.

3. Nine hundred thousand Vipers blue, he charm'd, with sweet discourses,
And dined on them at Killaloe, in soups and second courses,
When blindworms crawling in the grass, disgusted all the nation,
He made them arise, and op'd their eyes to a sense of their situation.

4. No wonder then our Irish Boys should be so free and frisky,
For St. Patrick taught them first the joys of tipling the Whiskey.
No wonder that the Saint himself to taste it, should be willing,
For his Mother kept a Sheban Shop in the town of Enniskillin.

5. The Wicklow hills are very high, and so's the hill of Heath Sir,
But there's a hill much higher still, ay'e higher than them both Sir,
'Twas on the top of this high hill St. Patrick preach'd the Sarment
He drove the Frogs into the bogs, and bother'd all the Varment.

THE GIRL I LEFT BEHIND ME.

Moderato.
1. I'm lone - some since I cross'd the hills And o'er the moor that's sed - gy; With heav - y thought my
heart is fill'd Since I part - ed with Peg - gy. Whene'er I turn to view the place, The tears doth fall and
blind me, When I think on the charming grace Of the girl I left be - hind me.

2. The hours I remember well,
Which next to see doth move me,
The burning flames my heart doth tell,
Since first she owned she loved me.
In search of some one fair and gay,
Several doth remind me:
I know my darling loves me well,
Though I left her behind me.

3. The bees shall lavish, make no store,
And the dove become a ranger,
The fallen water cease to roar,
Before I'll ever change her.
Each mutual promise faithful made,
By her whose tears doth blind me,
And bless the hours I pass away,
With the girl I left behind me.

4. My mind her image full retains,
Whether asleep or awaken'd;
I hope to see my jewel again,
For her my heart is breaking.
But if ever I do go that way,
And she has not resigned me,
I'll reconcile my mind and stay
With the girl I left behind me.

CROOSKEEN LAWN.

3. Then fill your glasses high, let's not part with lips adry,
Tho' the lark now proclaims it is dawn;
And since we can't remain, may we shortly meet again,
To fill another crooskeen lawn, &c.
Gramachree ma crooskeen, &c.

4. And when grim Death appears, after few, but happy years,
And tells me my glass is run,
I'll say, "Be gone you slave, for great Bacchus gives me leave,
To drink another crooskeen lawn, &c.
Gramachree ma crooskeen, &c.

CROOSKEEN LAWN.

(ANOTHER VERSION.)

COMIN' THRO' THE RYE.

The original words of "Comin' thro' the Rye" cannot be satisfactorily traced. There are many different versions of the song. The following is the one most approved, and generally sung. The air forms, with slight variation, the third and fourth strains of the strathspey called "The Miller's Daughter."

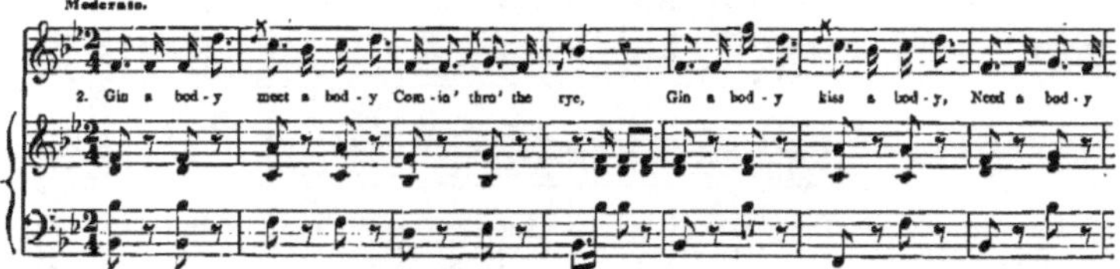
Moderato.
2. Gin a bod - y meet a bod - y Com - in' thro' the rye, Gin a bod - y kiss a bod - y, Need a bod - y

cry? Ev - ery lass - ie has her lad - die: Nane, they say, hae I; Yet a' the lads they smile at me, When comin' thro' the
p

rye. A - mang the train there is a swain I dear - ly lo'e my - sel', But whaur his hame, or what his name, I dinna care to tell.
p

2 Gin a body meet a body
Comin' frae the town,
Gin a body greet a body,
Need a body frown?
Every lassie, &c.

One of the original verses.

Gin a body meet a body
Comin' frae the well,
Gin a body kiss a body—
Need a body tell?

Ilka Jenny has her Jocky,
Ne'er ane ha'e I;
But a' the lads they look at me—
And what the waur am I?

JOHN ADERSON MY JO, JOHN.

Written by Burns.

2 John Anderson, my jo, John, we clamb the hill thegither,
And mony a canty day, John, we've had wi' ane anither;
Now we maun totter down, John, but hand in hand we'll go,
And we'll sleep thegither at the foot, John Anderson, my jo.

3 John Anderson my jo, John, ye were my first conceit,
And ye maunna think it strange, John, though I ca' ye trim and neat;
Though some folk think ye're auld, John, I never think ye so,
But I think ye're a' the same to me, John Anderson, my jo.

4 John Anderson, my jo, John, we've seen our bairns' bairns;
And yet, my dear John Anderson, I'm happy in your arms;
And sae are ye in mine, John,—I'm sure ye'll ne'er say no,
Though the days are gane that we have seen, John Anderson my jo.

5 John Anderson my jo, John, what pleasure does it gie
To see sae mony sprouts, John, spring up 'tween you and me!
And ilka lad and lass, John, in our footsteps to go,
Makes perfect heaven here on earth, John Anderson my jo.

6 John Anderson my jo, John, when we were first acquent,
Your locks were like the raven, your bonnie brow was brent;
But now your head's turn'd bauld, John, your locks are like the snaw,
Yet blessings on your frosty pow, John Anderson my jo.

7 John Anderson my jo, John, frae year to year we've pass'd,
And soon that year maun come, John, will bring us to our last;
But let na' that affright us, John, our hearts were ne'er our foe,
While in innocent delight we lived, John Anderson my jo.

FLOW GENTLY, SWEET AFTON.*

Words by ROBERT BURNS. Music by J. E. SPILMAN.

Andante.
1. Flow gently, sweet Afton, among thy green braes, Flow gently, I'll sing thee a song in thy praise; My Mary's a-sleep by thy
murmuring stream; Flow gently, sweet Afton, disturb not her dream. Thou stock-dove, whose echo resounds through the glen, Ye wild whistling
blackbirds, in yon flowery den, Thou green-crested lapwing, thy screaming for - bear, I charge you, disturb not my slumbering fair.

2

How lofty, sweet Afton, thy neighbouring hills,
Far mark'd with the courses of clear winding hills;
There daily I wander, as morn rises high,
My flocks and my Mary's sweet cot in my eye.
How pleasant thy banks and green valleys below,
Where wild in the woodlands the primroses blow;
There oft, as mild evening creeps o'er the lea,
The sweet-scented birk shades my Mary and me.

3

Thy crystal stream, Afton, how lovely it glides,
And winds by the cot where my Mary resides!
How wanton thy waters her snowy feet lave,
As, gath'ring sweet flow'rets, she stems thy clear wave!
Flow gently, sweet Afton, among thy green braes;
Flow gently, sweet river, the theme of my lays;
My Mary's asleep by thy murmuring stream,
Flow gently, sweet Afton, disturb not her dream.

* This is sung in Scotland to the tune of "The Yellow-Haired Laddie." See opposite page.

DAINTY DAVIE.

Written by Burns.

ain dear dain - ty Da - vie.

2 When purple morning starts the hare,
I'o steal upon her early fare,
Then through the dews I will repair,
To meet my faithfu' Davie.

When day, expiring in the west,
The curtain draws o' Nature's rest,
I'll flee to his arms I lo'e best,
And that's my dainty Davie.

BONNIE DUNDEE.

Written by Sir Walter Scott.

Spirited, but not too fast.
1. To the lords of convention 'twas Claverhouse spoke, Ere the king's crown go down there are crowns to be broke, So each ca - va - lier who loves honor and me, Let him fol-low the bonnet of bonnie Dundee. Come, fill up my cup, come, fill up my can, Come, saddle my horses and call up my men, Come, o - pen the west port and let me gae free, And its room for the bonnets of bon-nie Dundee.
2. Dundee he is mounted, he rides up the street, The bells are rung backward, the drums they are beat, But the Provost, douce man, said just e'en let him be, The town is weel quit of that deil of Dundee. Come, fill up, &c.
3. There are hills beyond Pentland, and streams beyond Forth, If there's lords in the Southland there's chiefs in the North, There are wild dunnie wassals three thousand times three Will cry "Hey for the bonnets of bonnie Dundee." Come fill up, &c.
4. A-wa' to the hills, to the woods, to the rocks, Ere I own a u - surp - er I'll couch with the fox, And tremble, false Whigs, tho' tri-umphant ye be, You have not seen the last of my bonnet and me. Come, fill up, &c.
Cres.

THE ROSE OF ALLANDALE.

1. The morn was fair, the skies were clear, No breath came o'er the sea, When Ma - ry left her Highland cot, and
wan-dered forth with me; Though flow - - - ers deck'd the moun - tain's side, And fra - grance fill'd the vale, By
far the sweetest flow - er there, Was the Rose of Al - lan - dale, Was the Rose of Al - lan - dale the
Rose of Al - lan - dale, By far the sweet - est flow-er there was the Rose of Al - lan - dale.

2 Where'er I wander'd east or west,
Though fate began to low'r,
A solace still was she to me,
In sorrow's lonely hour;
When tempest's lash'd our gallant bark
And rent her shiv'ring sail,
One maiden form withstood the storm,
'Twas the Rose of Allandale, &c.

3 And when my fever'd lips were parch'd
On Afric's burning sand,
She whispers hopes of happiness,
And tales of distant lands;
My life had been a wilderness,
Unblest by fortune's gale,
Had fate not link'd my lot to hers,
The Rose of Allandale, &c.

THE BLUE BELL OF SCOTLAND.

Words by Mrs. Grant of Laggan.

2 O where, tell me where, did your Highland laddie stay?
O where, tell me where, did your Highland laddie stay?
He dwelt beneath the holly trees, beside the rapid Spey,
And many a blessing follow'd him the day he went away.

3 O what, tell me what, does your Highland laddie wear?
O what, tell me what, does your Highland laddie wear?
A bonnet with a lofty plume, the gallant badge of war,
And a plaid across the manly breast that yet shall wear a star.

4 Suppose, ah suppose, that some cruel, cruel wound
Should pierce your Highland laddie, and all your hopes confound!
The pipe would play a cheering march, the banners round him fly,
The spirit of a Highland chief would lighten in his eye.

5 But I will hope to see him yet in Scotland's bonnie bounds,
But I will hope to see him yet in Scotland's bonnie bounds,
His native land of liberty shall nurse his glorious wounds,
While wide through all our Highland hills his warlike name resounds.

The following is another version of the song:

1 Oh where, and oh where, is your Highland laddie gone?
Oh where, and oh where, is your Highland laddie gone?
He's gone to fight the French for King George upon his throne,
And it's oh, in my heart I wish him safe at home.

2 Oh where, and oh where, did your Highland laddie dwell?
Oh where, and oh where, did your Highland laddie dwell?
He dwelt in merry Scotland, at the sign of the Blue Bell;
And its oh, in my heart I love my laddie well.

3 In what clothes, in what clothes, is your Highland laddie clad?
In what clothes, in what clothes, is your Highland laddie clad?
His bonnet's of the saxon green, and his vest is of the plaid,
And it's oh, in my heart I love my Highland lad.

4 Suppose, and suppose, that your Highland lad should die?
Suppose, and suppose, that your Highland lad should die?
The bagpipes should play over him, I'd sit me down and cry;
And its oh, in my heart I hope he will not die.

A MAN'S A MAN FOR A' THAT.

Written by BURNS, in 1794, and sent to Thompson's Collection with the following observations: "A great critic (Aikin) on songs, says that love and wine are the exclusive themes for song-writing. The following is on neither subject, and consequently is no song, but will be allowed, I think, to be two or three pretty good prose thoughts inverted into rhyme."

Moderato con espressione.
Is there for hon-est pov-er-ty, That hangs his head, and a' that? The cow-ard slave, we pass him by; We dare be puro for a' that. For a' that, and a' that, Our toils ob-scure, and a' that; The rank is but the guinea stamp; The man's the gowd, for a' that.

2

What though on hamely fare we dine,
Wear hodden gray, and a' that;
Gie fools their silks, and knaves their wine;
A man's a man for a' that.
For a' that, and a' that,
Their tinsel show, and a' that;
The honest man, though e'er sae puir,
Is king o' men, for a' that.

3

Ye see yon birkie, ca'd a lord,
Wha struts and stares, and a' that;
Though hundreds worship at his word,
He's but a cuif for a' that.
For a' that, and a' that,
His ribbon, star and a' that,
The man of independent mind,
He looks and laughs at a' that.

4

A king can make a belted knight,
A marquis, duke, and a' that;
But an honest man's a boon his might,
Gude faith, he maunna fa' that!
For a' that, and a' that,
Their dignities, and a' that,
The pith o' sense, the pride o' worth,
Are higher ranks than a' that.

5

Then let us pray that come it may,
As come it will for a' that,
That sense and worth, o'er a' the earth,
May bear the gree, and a' that.
For a' that, and a' that,
It's coming yet, for a' that,
That man to man, the world o'er,
Shall brithers be, for a' that.

THE AULD GREY KIRK.

2 Yestreen we met beside the birk,
A-down ayont the burnie O;
An' wan'er't, till the auld gray kirk
A stap put to our journey O;
"Ah, lassie! there it stan's," quo' I,
"Can crown our earthly blisses" O,
Syne smoor't fu' sweetly a' reply,
An' conquer't her wi' kisses O.

3 I had her heart—she gae her han'—
The burnin' blush was spreadin' O;
She lean't my 'raptured breast upon,
While floods o' joy were sheddin' O;
Tho guid! the best! she's a' my ain—
Our fates thegither seal't we O;
An' I—may foulest fate be mine,
Gin I forget my fealty O.

LEWIE GORDON.

(A Jacobite Song.) Words by Dr. Alexander Geddes.

The Lewis Gordon alluded to was third son to the Duke of Gordon. He declared for Prince Charles on the rising in 1745, and was afterwards attainted, but escaped to France, where he died in 1754.

Andante.
1. The bonnie bonnie bairn, who sits
mf
1. O send Lewie Gordon hame, And the lad I daurna name;
Though his back be at the wa', Here's to him that's far a-wa'!
f
O-chon, my Highlandman! O my bonnie Highlandman!
Weel would I my true love ken, Among ten thousand Highlandmen.

2 O! to see his tartan trews,
Bonnet blue, and laigh-heeled shoes,
Philabeg aboon his knee!
That's the lad that I'll gang wi'.
Ochon, &c.

3 This lovely youth of whom I sing,
Is fitted for to be a king;
On his breast he wears a star;
You'd tak' him for the god of war.
Ochon, &c.

4 O! to see this princely one
Seated on a royal throne!
Disasters a' would disappear;
Then begins the jub'lee year.
Ochon, &c.

CASTLES IN THE AIR.

2

He sees muckle castles towering to the moon!
He sees little sodgers pu'ing them a' doun!
Worlds whombling up and doun, bleezing wi' a flare,
See how he loups! as they glimmer in the air.
For a' sae sage he looks, what can the laddie ken?
He's thinking upon naething, like mony mighty men;
A wee thing mak's us think, a sma' thing mak's us stare,
There are mair folk than him bigging castles in the air.

3

Sic a night in winter may weel mak' him cauld;
His chin upon his buffy hand will soon mak' him auld;
His brow is brent sae braid, O pray that daddy Care
Would let the wean alane wi' his castles in the air!
He'll glower at the fire! and he'll keek at the light!
But mony sparkling stars are swallow'd up by night;
Aulder een than his are glamoured by a glare,
Hearts are broken, heads are turn'd, wi' castles in the air.

WILLIE BREW'D A PECK O' MAUT.

Written by BURNS, in 1789, and set to music by ALLAN MASTERTON. It has been pronounced the best of all Burns's bacchanalian pieces. The meeting which it celebrates took place between the poet, William Nichol, of the High School, Edinburgh, and Allan Masterton, another schoolmaster and musical amateur. Nichol had bought a small farm, named "Laggan," in the parish of Dunscore, Dumfriesshire, where he spent the autumn vacations. Masterton and Burns went on a visit to the "illustrious lord of Laggan's many hills." Nichol, as in duty bound, produced his best. Tradition asserts, that day dawned long ere the guests arose to depart.

1. O, Willie brew'd a peck o' maut, And Rob and Al - lan
cam' to prie; Three blither lads, that lee lang night, Ye wad - na find in Christendie. We are na fou, we're
no that fou, But just a wee drap in our e'e; The cock may craw, the day may daw, But aye we'll taste the barley bree.

2

Here are we met, three merry boys;
Three merry boys, I trow, are we;
And mony a nicht we've merry been,
And mony mo'e we hope to be.
We are nae fou, &c.

3

It is the mune—I ken her horn,
That's blinkin' in the lift sae hie;
She shines sae bricht to wyle us hame;
But, by my sooth, she'll wait awee.
We are nae fou, &c.

4

Wha first shall rise to gang awa',
A cuckold, coward loun is he;
Wha last beside his chair shall fa',
He is the king amang us three.
We are nae fou, &c.

ROY'S WIFE OF ALDIVALLOCH.

Words by Mrs. Grant, of Leggan.

Andantino, quasi Allegretto.
1. Roy's wife of Al - di - val - loch, Roy's wife of Al - di - val - loch, wat ye how she cheat - ed me? As
I came o'er the braes of Bal - loch, She vow'd, she swore she wad be mine, She said that she loe'd me
Fine.
best of o - ny, But O the fick - le faith - less queen, She's ta'en the carl, and left her John - ie.
D.C.
D.C.

2 O she was a canty quean,
And weel cou'd she dance the Highland walloch;
How happy I, had she been mine,
Or I'd been Roy of Aldivalloch.

3 But Roy's age is three times mine,
I think his days will nae be mony,
And when the carl is dead and gane,
She'll may be rue and take her Johnny.

4 Her hair so fair, her e'en sae clear,
Her wee bit mou' sae sweet and bonny;
To me she ever will be dear,
Tho' she's forever left her Johnie.

WANDERING WILLIE.

Burns, who was fond of the tune of "Here awa, there awa," wrote the following fine verses to it, in March, 1797.

2 Winter winds blew loud and cauld at our parting;
Fears for my Willie brought tears in my e'e:
Welcome now, summer, and welcome my Willie,
The summer to nature, and Willie to me.

3 Rest, ye wild storms, in the caves of your slumbers!
How your dread howling a lover alarms!
Wauken, ye breezes! row gently, ye billows!
And waft my dear laddie ance mair to my arms.

4 But, oh, if he's faithless, and minds na his Nannie,
Flow still between us, thou dark heaving main!
May I never see it, may I never trow it,
But, dying, believe that my Willie's my ain.

HERE AWA', THERE AWA'.

The beautiful air of "Here awa', there awa'," is preserved in Oswald's Collection of Scots' Tunes, 1735–42. Herd, in his Collection of 1769, first printed the following fragment of the old words.

1 Here awa', there awa', here awa', Willie!
'Here awa', there awa', haud awa', hame!
Lang have I sought thee, dear have I bought thee,
Now I have gotten my Willie again.

2 Through the lang muir I have followed my Willie;
Through the lang muir I have followed him hame;
Whatever betide us, nought shall divide us;
Love now rewards all my sorrow and pain.

3 Here awa', there awa', here awa', Willie!
Here awa', there awa', haud awa', hame!
Come, love, believe me, nothing can grieve me,
Ilka thing pleases when Willie's at hame.

ANDRO AND HIS CUTTY GUN.*

2 She took me in, and set me down,
And heckt to keep me lawing free
But, cunning carline that she was,
She gaut me biol my bawbee.

3 We loo'd the liquor well enough;
But waes my heart, my cash was done,
Before that I had quench'd my drouth,
And laith I was to pawn my shoon.

4 When we had three times toom'd our stoup,
And the neist chappin new begun,
Wha started in, to heeze our hope,
But Andro wi' his cutty gun.

5 The carline brought her kebbuck ben,
With girdle-cakes weel toasted broun;
Weel does the canny kimmer ken
They gar the swatsgoe glibber down.

6 We ca'd the bicker aft about;
Till dauning we ne'er ee'd our bun,
And aye the cleanest drinken out,
Was Andro wi' his cutty gun.

7 He did like any mavis sing,
And as I in his oxter sat,
He ca'd me aye his bonnie thing,
And mony a sappy kiss I got.

8 I ha'e been east, I ha'e been west,
I ha'e been far ayont the sun;
But the blythest lad that e'er I saw,
Was Andro wi' his cutty gun.

* "This blythsome song," says Burns, "so full of Scottish humor and convivial merriment, is an intimate favorite at bridal trystes and house-heatings. It contains a spirited picture of a country alehouse, touched off with all the lightsome gaiety so peculiar to the rural muse of Scotland." Elsewhere, in a letter to Thomson, (Nov. 19, 1794,) "Andro and his cutty gun" is the work of a master." A "Hawick gill," alluded to in the chorus, was a double gill; a "tappit-hen," was a quart stoup with a knob on the top of the lid.

BLYTHE. BLYTHE AND MERRY WAS SHE.

Written by Burns, in 1718, to the tune of "Andro and his cutty gun," and published in the second vol. of Johnson's Museum. "I composed these verses," says the poet, "while I stayed at Auchtertyre with Sir Wm. Murray." The heroine was "Miss Euphemia Murray, commonly and deservedly called The Flower of Strathmore;" she was married, in 1794, to Lord Methven, a Judge in the Court of Session.

1 Blythe, blythe and merry was she,
Blythe was she but and ben;
B'ythe by the banks of Earn,
And blythe in Glenturit glen.
By Ochtertyre grows the silk,
On Yarrow braes the birken shaw;
But Phemie was a bonnier lass
Than braes o'Yarrow ever saw.

2 Her looks were like a flower in May
Her smile was like a simmer morn;
She tripped by the banks o' Earn,
As light's a bird upon a thorn.

3 Her bonnie face, it was as meek
As onie lamb upon a lee;
The evening sun was ne'er sae sweet
As was the blink o' Phemie's e'e.

4 The Highland hills I've wander'd wide,
And o'er the Lowlands I ha'e been;
But Phemie was the blythest lass
That ever trod the dewy green.

MARY OF ARGYLE.

O, WHISTLE, AND I'LL COME TO YOU, MY LAD.

Written by Burns, in 1793, to an old air composed by John Bruce, a famous fiddler in Dumfries, about the middle of the last century.

2

Come down the back stairs when you come to court me,
Come down the back stairs when you come to court me,
Come down the back stairs, and let naebody see,
And come as ye were na coming to me.
O, whistle, &c.

3

At kirk or at market, whene'er ye meet me,
Gang by me as though that he cared na a flie;
But steal me a blink o' your bonnie blue e'e,
Yet look as ye were na lookin' at me.
O, whistle, &c.

4

Aye, vow and protest that ye care na for me,
And whyles ye may lichtly my beauty a wee;
But court na anither, though jokin ye be,
For fear that she wyle your fancy frae me.
O, whistle, &c.

O JEAN, I LOVE THEE.

Poetry by Burns. Collated by Kotzeluch.

2

Then come, sweet Muse, inspire my lay;
For, a' the lee-lang simmer's day,
I couldna sing, I couldna say,
  How much, how dear I love thee.
I see thee dancing ower the green,
Thy waist sae jimp, thy limbs sae clean,
Thy tempting lips, thy roguish een—
  By heaven and earth, I love thee.

3

By night, by day, a-field, at hame—
The thoughts of thee my breast inflame!
And aye I muse and sing thy name—
  I only live to love thee.
Though I were doom'd to wander on,
Beyond the sea, beyond the sun,
Till my last weary sand was run,
  Till then—and then I'll love thee.

SCOTS, WHA HA'E WI' WALLACE BLED!

AIR—"Hey, tuttie taitie."

2

Wha will be a traitor knave?
Wha will fill a coward's grave?
Wha sae base as be a slave?
  Let him be a slave!
Wha, for Scotland's king and law,
Freedom's sword will strongly draw,
Freeman stand, or freeman fa',
  Let him follow me!

3

By oppression's woes and pains,
By your sons in servile chains,
We will drain our dearest veins,
  But they shall be free.
Lay the proud usurpers low!
Tyrants fall in every foe!
Liberty's in every blow!
  Let us do or die!

KINLOCH OF KINLOCH; or, THE CHEVALIER'S LAMENT.

Written by Burns.

2

The deed that I dared could it merit their malice,
A king and a father to place on his throne;
His right are those hills, and his right are these valleys,
Where the wild beasts find shelter, but I can find none.
But what can, &c.

3

But 'tis not my sufferings—thus wretched, forlorn,
My brave gallant friends, 'tis your ruin I mourn;
Your deeds proved so loyal in hot bloody trial,
Alas! can I make it no better return?
But what can, &c.

WITHIN A MILE OF EDINBURG TOWN.

1. 'Twas with - in a mile of Ed - in - bor - o' town, In the ro - sy time of the year, Sweet flow - ers bloom'd and the
2. Jock - y was a wag that nev - er would wed, Tho' long he had followed the lass, Contented she earned and eat
3. But when he vow'd he would make her his bride, Tho' his flocks and his herds were not few, She gave him her hand and a

grass was down, And each shep-herd woo'd his dear; Bonny Jocky, blithe and gay, Kiss'd sweet Jenny makin' hay, The
her own bread; And merrily turned up the grass. Bonny Jocky, blithe and free, Won her heart right mer-ri - ly; Yet
kiss be - side, And vow'd she'd forever be true. Bonny Jocky, blithe and free, Won her heart right mer-ri - ly; At

lassie blush'd and frowning cried, No, no, it will not do, ... I cannot, cannot, wonnot, wonnot, monnot buckle to.
still she blush'd and frowning cried, No, no, it will not do, ... I cannot, &c.
church she no more frowning cried, No, no, it will not do, ... I cannot, &c.

TO DAUNTON ME.*

The tune of "Daunton me" is to be found in Oswald, (1740). The following words are chiefly by Burns, and were written by him for Johnson's Museum. Part of the chorus and some of the rest of the words are old.

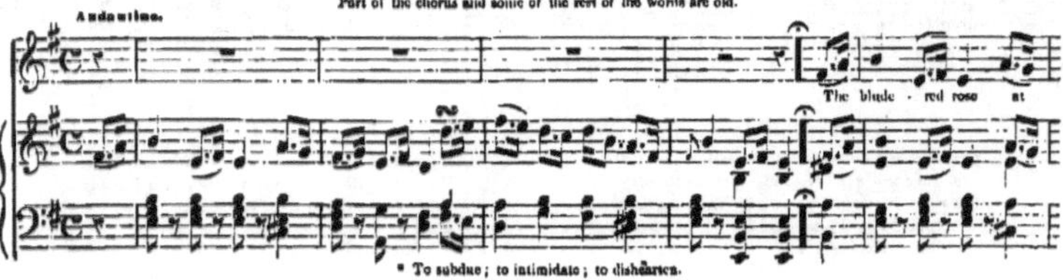

Andantino.
The blude - red rose at

* To subdue; to intimidate; to dishearten.

Yule may blaw, The sum - mer lil - lies bloome in snaw, The frost may freeze the deep - est sea; But an
auld man nev - er shall daun - ton me! To daun - ton me, and me sae young, Wi' his fause heart and
flat - tering tongue! That is the thing ye ne'er shall see; For an auld man ne'er shall daun - ton me.

2 For a' his meal, for a' his maut,
For a' his fresh beef and his saut,
For a' his gowd and white monie,
An auld man ne'er shall daunton me.—Cho.

3 His gear may buy him kye and yowes,
His gear may buy him glens and knowes:
But me he shall not buy nor fee;
For an auld man ne'er shall daunton me.—Cho.

4 He hirples twa-fauld, as he dow,
Wi' his teethless gab and auld bauld pow.
And the rain rins doun frae his red-bleared e'e;
That auld man ne'er shall daunton me.—Cho.

JACOBITE VERSION, FROM HOGG'S "JACOBITE RELIQUES."

1 To daunton me, and me sae young,
And guid king James's auldest son!
O, that's the thing that ne'er can be;
For the man is unborn that'll daunton me.
O, set me ance on Scottish land,
My guid braidsword into my hand,
My blue bonnet abune my bree,—
And shaw me the man that'll daunton me.

2 It's nae the battle's deadly stoure,
Nor friends proved false, that'll gaur me cower;
But the reckless hand o' povertie,
O, that alane can daunton me.
High was I born to kingly gear,
But a cuif cam' in my cap to wear;
But wi' my broadsword I'll let him see
He's nae the man to daunton me.

3 O, I ha'e scarce to lay me on,
Of kingly fields were ance my ain,
Wi' the muir-cock on the mountain bree;
But hardship ne'er can daunton me.
Up cam' the gallant chief Lochiel,
And drew his glaive o' nut-brown steel,
Says, Charlie, set your fit to me,
And shaw me wha will daunton thee?

THE YELLOW-HAIRED LADDIE.

Written by Allan Ramsay.

Andante.
1. In A-pril, when prim-ro-ses paint the sweet plain, And sum-mer, ap-proach-ing, re-joic-eth the swain, The yel-low-haired lad-die would oft-en times go To woods and deep glens, where the haw-thorn trees grow. haw-thorn trees grow.
tr
1st time.
2d time.

2

There, under the shade of an old sacred thorn,
With freedom he sung his loves evening and morn;
He sung with so soft and enchanting a sound,
That sylvans and fairies unseen danced around.

3

The shepherd thus sung, "Though young Maddie be fair,
Her beauty is dash'd with a scornful, proud air;
But Susie was handsome, and sweetly could sing,—
Her breath's like the breezes perfumed in the spring.

4

That Maddie, in all the gay bloom of her youth,
Like the moon was inconstant, and never spoke truth;
But Susie was faithful, good-humored and free,
And fair as the goddess that sprung from the sea.

5

That mamma's fine daughter, with all her great dower,
Was awkwardly airy, and frequently sour."
Then sighing, he wished, would but parents agree,
That witty, sweet Susan his mistress might be.

PARTING WALTZES.

(SCHEIDEN.)

E. WEISSENDORN.

Published in Quintette Quadrille Band Book, No. 2.

ff
fz
No. 3.
p
f
ff
No. 4.
p
dim.

FINE.
ff
fz
ff
fz
ff
fz
dim.
D.C.
No. 5.
decres.
p

LET'S BE GAY WALTZES.

JOSEF STRAUSS.

(LUSTSCHWÄRMER.)

Published in Quintette Quadrille Band, No. 2.

No. 1.

No. 3.

f
p
No. 5.
p
p
p
f
dim.
pp

DREAM ON THE OCEAN WALTZES.

JOSEF GUNG'L.

No. 1.

No. 2.

No. 3.
Cres.
Cres.
Cres.

No. 4.
p
Dim.
ff
p
Dim.
ff
Ped.
p
ff
Ped.
1
2
f
No. 5.
p
Cres.
ff
Ped.
pp

HILDA WALTZES.

D. GODFREY.

ff

I II D.C.

No. 3.

2d time in Octaves.

Cres.

FINE. 2d time. *fp* *ff*

D.C.

No. 4.
p
f
THE PERI WALTZES.
C. D'ALBERT.
No. 1.
p
Cres.
FINE.
ff
Ped.
Ped.
D.C.

No. 2.
f
p
cres
ff
I
II
ff
I
II
No. 3.
f
p
f
p
ff
FINE.
ff
p
ff
ff
D.C.

VILLAGE SWALLOWS WALTZES.

JOSEF STRAUSS.

(DORFSCHWALBEN AUS OSTERREICH.)

No. 1.

p
f
Dim.
pp
No. 3.
f
f
Fine.
f
D.C.
No. 4.

f
f
f
No. 5.
p
pp
Bis.
pp
mf f
ff
pp
f

ADELE WALTZES.

D. GODFREY.

sf
p
ff
D.C.
No. 3.
8va 2d time.
p
sf
ff

D.C.
No. 4.
p
f
f
ff

NATHALIE WALTZES.

LABITZKY.

sf
sf
p
f
p
f
No. 3.
p
Ped.
f
p
f
p
ff
Ped.
*
Ped.
*
p

No. 4.
p
Ped.
Ped.
Ped.
Ped.
No. 5.
ff
p
f
Fine.
Ped.
ff
D.S. Al fine.

WOODLAND WHISPERS WALTZES.

GERALD STANLEY

No. 3.
1
2
No. 4.

THE BRIDESMAID WALTZES.

CHARLES COOTE, JUN.

No. 3.
p
f
No. 4.
ff
mf

I
II
last
MABEL WALTZES.
D. GODFREY.
No. 1.
2d time in Octaves.
p
2d time in Octaves.
FINE.
p
f
I
II
D.C.

No. 2.
2d. time in Octaves.
FINE.
D.C.
No. 3.
FINE.

ff
ff
D.C.
No. 4.
ff
p
ff
p
f
ff

GOVERNOR SPRAGUE'S GRAND MARCH.

E. MACK.

ff

ff

FINE.

TRIO.

p

ff

D. AL TRIO, then D. C.

IDA GALOP.

(FRAÜLEIN BRADE ZUGEEIGNET.)

C. FAUST.

FINE.
TRIO.
p
f
ff
D.C. to GALOP.
OVER STICKS AND STONES GALOP.
(UEBER STOCK UND STEIN.)
C. FAUST.
ff
p
ff

TRIO.
p
f
FINE.
tr
ff
p

THROUGH THE AIR GALOP.

C. FAUST.

D.C. Al fine.
STORM BIRD GALOP.
(DER STURM VOGEL.)
C. FAUST.

STORM BIRD GALOP. Concluded.

mf
p
mf
ff
mf
ff
sfmf
D.C.
TRIO.
p
f
p
f
p
p

COLUMBANUS GALOP.

ALBERT PARLOW.

INTRODUCTION.

GALOP.

FINE.

TRIO.
p
ff
tr
tr
tr
DAL TRIO. THEN D.C. TO GALOP AL FINE.

GRANDE DUCHESSE QUADRILLE.

STRAUSS.

D.C.
All hands around that couple.
No. 3.
(Fritz's complaint.)
All forward and back.
Half right and left.
First two right hands across.
Back with left.
CODA.
FINE.
Balance.
Half promenade.
4 times.
Ladies chain.
D.C.
No. 4.
FINE.
Four hands half right and left.
Half right and left to place.

First couple forward.
Leave the lady opposite.
Forward and back.
Ladies cross over.
D.C.
Forward and back twice.
All hands around.
No. 5.
All balance to partners and turn.
(Sabre song.)
FINE.
Ladies balance to right.
Turn.
Balance to seat.
Turn.

No. 1.
FINE.
D.C.
D.C. AL FINE.
1st 4 Right and left, Balance, Ladies chain, Promenade.
No. 2.
Fine.
D.S. AL FINE.
Forward 2, Cross over. Chassez back and stop in the centre, 6 hands round to place.

No. 3.
POCO A POCO. CRESC.
1st 2 give right hand across, left hand back, Balance, Half promenade, Ladies Chain Forward, Half right and left to place.
No. 4.
FINE.
D.C. AL FINE.
1st couple lead to right, 4 hands round, Right and left with next couple, Ladies chain with next, All promenade.

1st 4 balance and turn; Forward and back, half right and left; Balance and turn: Forward and back, half right and left to place. 1st 4 polka. Sides polka. All polka.

f
mf
tr
p
D.C.
1st couple polka inside.—Grand right and left half round; Polka to place.
Next couple, &c.
Next couple, &c.
Next couple, &c.
No. 3.
p
f
p
D.C.
All join hands, forward; ladies pass to right; all polka.
Four times; Last time all polka round the hall.

GOOD FOR THE TONGUE.

Form in sets of six couples. First and second couples cross over and down the outside (ladies on the gentlemen's side and gentlemen on the ladies side,) swing half round at the foot of the set, up the outside and cast off one couple, forward and back six, first two couples cross right hands half round, left hands back, right and left.
THE CUCKOO.
First lady down the outside, (gentleman crosses over and follows.) back up the middle, first gentleman down the outside, (lady crosses over and follows,) back up the middle, (join hands,) down the centre, back and cast off, right and left four.
CHORUS JIG.
Down the outside, up, down the middle, back, cast off, swing contra corners, balance, and swing to place.

LADY WALPOLE'S REEL. Music, Massai's Favorite.

ALLEGRO.
First couple join right hands and swing half round (first lady give left hand to second gentleman's right) (gentleman give his left hand to second lady's right) balance four in a line, first lady swing with second gentleman, first gentleman swing with second lady at the same time and pass partner.
Join hands again with second couple, balance four in a line, swing to places.
Down the centre with partner, up. (cast off.)
Right and left four.
MONEY MUSK.
First couple join right hands and swing once and a half round, go below second couple (the first lady goes below the second gentleman on the outside) (first gentleman at the same time goes below and between second and third ladies.)
Forward and back six, first couple swing three quarters round.
First gentleman goes between second couple (on the inside,) first lady goes between the second couple (on the inside) forward and back six, first couple swing three quarters round to place (below one couple.)
Right and left four.
DEVIL'S DREAM.
Form in sets of six couples.
First couple down the outside (foot couple up the centre same time) back first couple down the centre back and cast off (foot couple up the outside and back at the same time.)
Ladies chain first four.
Right and left.

COLLEGE HORNPIPE.
First lady balance to the third gentleman, turn the second gentleman—
First gentleman balance to third lady, turn with the second lady—
First couple down the centre, back (cast off)—
Right and left four.
DURANG'S HORNPIPE.
First lady balance with the second gentleman, turn with partner—
First gentleman balance with the second lady, turn with partner—
First couple down the centre, back, cast off one couple—
Right and left with the same.
FRED WILSON'S CLOG DANCE.
Figure—Six-handed Reel.
First couple cross over and go outside second couple, inside between second and third couple, pass outside of third couple up to head and back to places (as the first gent passes outside of second lady, she turns and follows, as he passes inside and around below third lady, she follows, thus the second and third lady make a straight right and left with each other). The gent now makes the same changes with the second and third gents, and the first lady at same time with second and third lady, first couple down the centre, back, cast off, right and left.
How to call Contra Dances — College Hornpipe for example.
The first change of "first lady balance to third gentleman, and turn the second gentleman," is called while the first strain, or first eight bars of music is played—the change of "first gentleman, &c.," is called while the first strain of music is repeated—the next change "the first couple down the centre and back, (cast off)—is called while the second strain of music is played—and the last change of "right and left four," is called while the last or second strain of music is repeated.

THE TEMPEST.
113
Form in two lines of six or eight couples on a side.
FINE.
First two couples down the centre (one couple from each line) four abreast, couples part at the foot and up abreast, and turn around opposite the next couple that was below them on starting.
Four on each side right and left.
D.C.
Ladies chain with the same couple.
Balance, four hands round (on each side) same four down the centre, &c.
THE FLOWERS OF EDINBURGH.
ALLEGRETTO.
First and foot couples balance to partners, first couples down the centre (foot couple up the outside at the same time.)
Same couples balance again, foot couple down the centre (first couple up the outside at the same time.)
First four ladies chain (foot four right and left at the same time) swing four hands half round and back at the head and foot of the set (at the same time) the same cross right hands half round, left hands back.
First two couples half promenade, first couple down the centre to foot and stop.
FISHER'S HORNPIPE.
First couple down the outside, up.
Down the centre, up (cast off.)
Swing six hands quite round.
Right and left.

VARSOVIENNE.

Slide the left foot forward; bring the right behind in the third position; spring out on the left foot, bringing the right foot up close; recommence the same with the right foot. This dance is composed of the same step as the Polka, with the exception that you slide the first step instead of springing, and omit the pause, as in this dance you count three, both for the music and dance.

This dance admits of various changes of direction.

ZULMA L'ORIENTALE.

The gentleman commences with the left foot and executes two Polka steps, turning round (which occupies 2 bars of music.)

Then place the point of the left foot in the fourth position (count one)—then bring the heel of the left foot back into the hollow of the right (third position—count two)—make a slight spring on the right foot and slide the left foot forward, bringing the right foot up behind the left in third position (count three)—then slide the left foot forward again and turn half round, finishing on the left foot with the right foot behind (count four)—occupying two bars. In all four bars.

For a lady the directions are the same, except reversing the feet.

DANISH DANCE.

This dance is of recent introduction in the first circles of society, and is a very pleasing one, combining the galop, two step waltz, and Schottisch turn. In the first place avoid stamping the first four steps, as it is exceedingly vulgar, and does not belong to the dance. Slide the left foot forward; then draw the right close up in the third position; perform this forward movement four times; then slide in the contrary direction, eight galop steps. Repeat the forward and back again, twice (16 bars). Then dance the two step waltz or the Schottisch; turn (16 bars), Then recommence with the first part.

LA HONGROISE.

Music LEONORA POLKA.

Hold your lady as usual—commence by holding up the left foot a little—then suddenly rise the right foot, and strike the heels together—then slide the left, and draw up the right to it, repeat this, which will complete two bars—then turn with the Pas de Basque, as in the Redowa, completing for bars—repeat the four bars,—then galop, eight bars,—then turn, four bars, and reverse, four bars—then backward and forward, striking the heels, and repeat the whole.

The music is in two-four time, slower then the Polka, yet somewhat lively.

No. 1. National Schottische.

No. 3. Flying Cloud Schottische.

LA TEMPETE.

CHARLES D'ALBERT.

Form as for a double Spanish dance.

All join hands fowarl and back, chassa by couples—All forward and back, all chassa by couples—couples two and three cross right hands half round, left hands back—(couples one and four at the same time) (each separately) join right hands, swing half round, left hands back. (couples two and three four hands half round and back) (couples one and four at the same time) each give hands half round and back—All forward and back, forward and pass through to next couples.

THE GERMAN REDOWA.

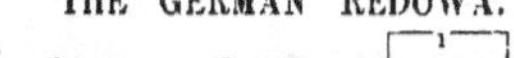

CHARLES D'ALBERT.

First four balance and turn—Forward and back—Half right and left—Balance and turn—Forward and back—Half right and left—First four polka—All polka—(Sides bal. &c. First couple polka in the centre—Grand right and left—All polka, (Other couples polka in centre, &c.) All join hands—Ladies pass to right—All polka—Four times, then all polka around the hall.

FIRST LOVE POLKA REDOWA.

(UN PREMIER AMOUR.)

WALLENSTEIN.

p FINE. *mf*

1st 4 balance and turn, Sides same, All polka redowa. 1st 4 polka redowa round,

D.C. TRIO. *p*

Half right and left, Sides the same.

f D.C.

1st 4 balance and turn, Sided polka round, Half right and left, Polka redowa to place.

ZULMA.

(NEW FANCY DANCE.)

mf

f D.C.

p D.C.

Standing in 1st position, rise on toe of left foot, at the same time place right foot in 2d position, bring left foot to 3d position, place right foot in 2d position again, rise on toe of right foot, and place left in 2d position, bring right foot to 3d position, place left foot in 2d position again; place right foot in 2d position, on the toes draw centre of same to left heel, glide right foot into 2d position, bring left foot to 3d, place right in 2d again, which finishes the step; Then commence other foot. Gentlemen will commence with the opposite foot.

PORTLAND FANCY.

Join hands and swing eight, head couple, (gentleman opposite lady,) down the middle, foot couple up the outside, (at the same time,) back to places; head couple down the outside, and foot couple up the middle, back to places: Ladies chain at the head, right and left at foot, right and left at head and ladies chain at foot, all forward, forward and cross by opposite couples and face the next four.

SICILLIAN CIRCLE

Form as for a Spanish dance—all balance—swing four hands—Ladies chain—balance and turn—right and left—all forward and back—forward again, pass to next couple. (One couple raise their hands, while the other stoops and passes through.)

DEMOCRATEN SCHOTTISCHE.

By permission of C. W. A, TRUMPLER, & Co.

TRIO.
mf
D.C.
VIOLETTA POLKA MAZURKA.
CARL FAUST.
mf
FINE.
ff
fz
D.C.
2nd time octave above.
TRIO.
p
f
f
ff
fz
fz
D.C. AL FINE.

ADELAIDE POLKA REDOWA.

HOWE'S
NEW SERIES OF MUSIC BOOKS,

PUBLISHED BY ELIAS HOWE,

NO. 103 COURT STREET, ... BOSTON.

PIANO MUSIC BOOKS.

[illegible]

VIOLIN, FLUTE, CLARIONET, FIFE, &c.

[illegible]

QUADRILLE AND BRASS BAND MUSIC.

[illegible]

ANY BOOK SENT BY MAIL ON RECEIPT OF PRICE.

www.ingramcontent.com/pod-product-compliance
Lightning Source LLC
Chambersburg PA
CBHW020120170426
43199CB00009B/577